Pam's Cooking

Marci Lynn McGuinness

with Pam Bendishaw

Pam's Cooking

©Shore Publications 2013

ISBN # 978-0-938833-50-5

Written by Marci Lynn McGuinness

with Pam Bendishaw

Shore Publications

145 River Street Adah, PA 15410.

724 710-2821

shorepublications@yahoo.com

www.ohiopyle.info

www.facebook.com/marcimcguinness

Cookery is not chemistry. It is an art. It requires instinct and taste rather than exact measurements.

– **Marcel Boulestin**

DEDICATION

As the author, I dedicate this book to my friend,
Pam Bendishaw of Hopwood, Pennsylvania. Her
talent and resilience has fed many a soul, and
employed a crew for many years. I thank you,
Pam, for being you. For always getting back up.
For being the hostess with more than the
mostess... For COOKING like only Pam can.

Thank you,
Marci McGuinness

Contents

ACKNOWLEDGMENTS

Thanks to Jay Lucky.
All Pam's faithful customers.
Bryce Bendishaw for his assistance.

No book about *Pam's Cooking* can be written without mentioning her late husband, Jimmy. "Bender" was a man who loved to eat and he married the right woman. I had many a meal with Pam and Jimmy at their home, Bender's Pit Stop and an array of restaurants through the years. Although he has been gone for six years, I still laugh at his antics.

Having dinner at Pam's kitchen table was always the best experience. The woman is literally, a cooking machine. Her stuffed pork chops will make you cry with joy.

The fun, laughter and fabulous food that Pam puts into motion are an extraordinary gift to us all. I honor not only her cooking, but her patience with those around her. For instance, one time we were eating at Back Bay in Morgantown. Pam ordered dessert, went to the restroom, and returned to an empty dessert plate and a smiling Jimmy. God Bless you, Pammy.

Appetizers &

Side Dishes

I want my Zucchini!

More Ranch, please.

Hand Cut French Fries

- Use a 90 count Idaho Potato.

- Cut the potato in half.

- Cut 16 fries, lengthwise, from the potato.

- Place fries in cold water and let stand for half an hour minimum. This removes the starch, allowing them to fry better.

- Drop in hot oil. Fry to golden brown.

  GREAT plain, but you can serve with ranch dressing, sprinkle with ®Old Bay Seasoning or top with chili and/or cheese sauce.

Hunger is the best sauce in the world.
-Cervantes

Potato Skins

- Use at least 4 - 90 count baking potatoes.

- 1lb fried crumbled bacon

- 2 cups shredded Cheddar cheese

- Sour cream

- Chives

- Bake potatoes 45 minutes and cool.

- Cut lengthwise.

- Scoop middle out leaving 1/8" of skin.

- Sprinkle bacon into each potato shell and fill with cheese.

- Bake at 350 degrees until cheese is melted.

- Top with sour cream and chives.

Steamed Shrimp

- Use raw shrimp in the shell - 16-20 size.

- Boil water seasoned with ®Old Bay. Add beer if desired.

- Boil shrimp one minute, remove and drain. Do not over cook!

- Sprinkle hot shrimp with Old Bay.

- Serve with cocktail sauce or drawn butter.

Cocktail Sauce: Mix ketchup with horseradish to your liking. Squeeze lemon juice into mix to taste.

Strip-Fried Zucchini

- Use medium-sized zucchini no longer than 12" and no bigger than 3" round.

- Use a meat slicer to slice very thin, lengthwise.

- Layer in a bucket: 2 sliced zucchini and salt, 2 sliced zucchini and salt, etc. Soak for an hour; toss while soaking to rotate evenly.

- An order for two is a handful. Rinse desired amount to fry. Place in a strainer and rinse. Gently squeeze excess water out of zucchini without harming it.

- Place in bowl of flour. Gently knead through fingers, dividing it so it does not stick together. Shake excess flour from zucchini.

- Drop into fryer. Shake it after a minute so it does not clump. Fry a little more and shake again.

- Serve with ranch dressing, horseradish sauce or marinara Sauce.

Stuffed Banana Peppers

- 4 dozen banana peppers (large) cut lengthwise and de-seeded

- 1 lb. grated Romano cheese

- 1 lb. shredded mozzarella

- 1 lb. shredded provolone

- 2 - 16 oz. cartons Ricotta cheese

- 3 eggs

- 1 cup Italian bread crumbs

- 2 oz. dried parsley

- Lay cut side up on cookie sheet coated with olive oil.

- Mix all other ingredients.

- Stuff peppers with cheese mix.

- Drizzle each with olive oil.

- Bake 400 degrees until cheese just begins to turn brown.

Stuffed Mushroom Caps

- 2lbs. sausage

- 1 Small onion – diced

- 4 Eggs

- 1 cup Italian bread crumbs

- Hot sauce (to taste)

- Shredded Mozzarella cheese (to taste)

- Your favorite mushrooms

- Wash mushrooms. Remove and dice stems.

- Mix well: sausage, onion, diced stems, eggs, bread crumbs, and hot sauce. Add salt and pepper to taste.

- Stuff mix into mushroom caps.

Bake at 350 degrees for 45 – 60 minutes.

Top with cheese the last 5 minutes.

I met Pam while working at Marc's Casual Dining in 1986. She had worked there before me and Marc told me she was coming back. Her son, Josh, was 15 months old. Marc described her to me like this, "You will love her. She is like you. You don't have to tell her what to do, she just does it".

We became instant friends. It took Jimmy and I a while to develop a kinship, but those stories will come out later, in my upcoming *Laurel Highland Legends* series.

Pam brought way more to the table at Marc's than the average waitress and cook. She perfected recipes and her warm heart and caring personality brought customers back constantly.

Pam took her cooking to Bender's Pit Stop when she and Jimmy opened up those doors. I thank you again, Pam, for giving of yourself so much. I give you, *Pam's Cooking*.

Soups

Crowd-Pleaser Pots of Soup

It's Chicken Noodle Day!

The discovery of a new dish does more for the happiness of mankind than the discovery of a star.

-Anthelme Brillat-Savarin

Cheesy Broccoli

- 2 stalks of celery chopped fine

- $\frac{1}{2}$ medium onion chopped fine

- 2 $\frac{1}{2}$ lb. bag of frozen broccoli florets

- $\frac{1}{2}$ lb. Butter

- 4-5 cups shredded Cheddar cheese

- Chicken base - 2 heaping tablespoons

- 2qts. heavy whipping cream or milk

Saute celery and onion in butter until caramelized. Add 64 oz. of water. Add broccoli. Boil. Add 64 more oz. of water. When hot add rue (flour whisked into water) and base to thicken. Add cheese and 1 qt. cream while stirring. Gradually add last qt. of cream to desired thickness.

Chicken Noodle

- 3 lbs. chicken breast – cooked and diced

- 3 lbs. chicken thighs – cooked and meat pulled from bone

- 2 gallons water

- 4 heaping tablespoons chicken base

- 2 large chopped carrots

- 3 stalks celery – diced

- 1 - 12 oz. Pkg. wide egg noodles

Put water in stock pot. Bring to boil. Stir in chicken base, celery and carrots. Add noodles and chicken. Season to taste. Cook until noodles are done.

Chicken & Dumpling

Same as Chicken Noodle except use dumplings instead of noodles.

Dumplings: Mix flour and egg together. Drop dumplings into soup.

Chili

- 1 large onion – cut in strips

- 2 large green peppers – chopped

- 2 large red peppers - chopped

- 5 lbs. ground chuck

- $\frac{1}{4}$ cup minced garlic

- 8 oz. chili powder

- Handful of hot pepper seeds – careful!

- 1 large banana pepper – diced

- Salt & pepper

- 128 oz. can kidney beans

- 128 oz. can diced tomatoes in juice

- 64 oz. water

Saute meat and vegetables until browned. Add beans, tomatoes and water. Bring to boil. Simmer.

Cream of Mushroom

- Celery – 2 stalks chopped fine

- $\frac{1}{2}$ medium onion – chopped fine

- 3lb. button mushrooms - chopped fine

- 64 oz. hot water

- Flour for rue

- 2qts. heavy whipping cream

- 2 heaping tablespoons chicken base

Brown celery, onions and mushrooms in stock pot in $\frac{1}{2}$ lb. butter. Cook until celery is done. Add 64 oz. water. Make rue with whisked flour and water and thicken soup with it. Add 1 qt. of cream at a time. Stir in the base and the last qt. of cream to desired thickness. Add more rue if needed. Makes 1 gallon.

Lima Bean & Ham

- 2 lbs. ham – diced

- 2 - 12 oz. bags large Lima beans

- ½ medium onion – chopped

- 2 heaping tablespoons chicken base.

- 2 sticks butter

Soak beans in water overnight. Drain. Cover beans with water and cook with butter until al dente. Add onion. Add water as needed. Add ham and chicken base. Stir. Add rue to thicken if needed. Add butter.

Only the pure in heart can make a good soup.

– **Ludwig van Beethoven**

Poor Man's Soup

- 4lb. hamburger

- 2 stalks celery – chopped

- $\frac{1}{2}$ med. onion chopped

- 3 tablespoons minced garlic

- 2- 64oz. cans seasoned diced tomatoes. Fill both cans with water.

- 1 lb. macaroni cooked, drained, rinsed.

- 2 Heaping tablespoons of beef base.

- Brown burger, onions, celery and garlic.

- Add tomatoes and water. Add beef base. Bring to boil. Simmer. Add salt & pepper to taste.

- Add cooked macaroni – use as much of the pound of macaroni as needed.

It is my belief that this soup cured my flu a few years ago!

Seafood Chowder

- 2lb. Whiting or any white fish -cubed

- 2lb. 21-25 size shrimp – peeled, tails off & cut in half

- 2lb. Bay scallops

- 1 – 64oz. can clam juice

- Small box of orzo – use $\frac{3}{4}$ of the box

- 2 – 64oz. cans seasoned (garlic/olive oil) diced tomatoes

- 64 oz. chicken broth

- Add to taste: ®Old Bay Seasoning, salt, pepper and granulated garlic.

Pour tomatoes, clam juice and chicken broth into large pot. Bring to boil. Add fish and orzo. Bring to boil for 15 minutes. Add scallops and shrimp. Season. Boil 5-8 minutes. Reduce to simmer. Taste and season accordingly. Add cayenne pepper for more spice.

-This recipe is in memory of Keith Fike.

Shrimp and Corn Chowder

- 7 medium peeled, diced potatoes

- ®Old Bay as needed. You want to taste it!

- 16 oz. roasted red peppers (drain) - diced

- 2 - 16 oz. cans corn

- Salt and pepper

- Chicken base – 2 heaping tablespoons

- 2 lbs. 21-25 size shrimp – peeled, cut in half

- Flour for rue

- 2 qts. heavy whipping cream

Cover potatoes with water and boil until tender. Reduce heat. Thicken potatoes with rue (flour & water, whisked). Stir in 1 qt. whipping cream. Bring to medium heat. Add 1 drained can of corn and one undrained can of corn. Add shrimp, peppers, base, seasoning. Slowly add last qt of cream. Add rue if needed to thicken.

Stuffed Pepper Soup

- Make your own (burger/rice) stuffed peppers (using ½ green bells and ½ red bells peppers)

- Bake them in 96 oz. ®Gia LaRusa Italian tomato sauce and 96 oz. basil seasoned-diced tomatoes.

- Chop them up. Heat in large pot.

Tomato Tortellini

- 2 - 64 oz. cans ®Campbell's tomato soup

- Fill one can with milk – add.

- Fill one can with water – add.

- Whisk while warming.

- Add 2 lbs. frozen cheese tortellini to soup and simmer

Vegetable Beef

- 2 lbs. stew meat

- 1 gallon water

- 1 small head of cabbage – chopped

- 2 – 64oz. cans diced tomatoes

- 8 medium peeled, diced potatoes

- 2 – 12oz. bags mixed frozen vegetables

- 2 heaping tablespoons of beef base.

Brown meat in butter in stock pot.

- Add water and cabbage. Add beef base. Boil until tender. Add water if needed.

- Add tomatoes, potatoes, and vegetables. Season with salt & pepper to taste.

- Simmer until tender.

Salads

Pam's Salads Have Personality!

Pam's base salad for chicken and steak salads:

Fill bowl ¾ full of chopped iceberg lettuce. Top with shredded carrots, diced beets, chopped onion, cucumbers, cherry tomatoes and shredded cheddar cheese. Pam's salad chicken or steak:

Grilled Chicken Salad

Pound out a chicken breast. Grill in a bit of olive oil. Cut into bite sized pieces as it cooks through.

Blackened Chicken Salad

Heat a cast iron skillet to 500 degrees. Season pounded chicken breast with ®Chef Paul Prudhomme's Seafood Magic. Place in hot skillet. Blacken. Cut into bite sized pieces as it cooks. WARNING: Do this outside on your grill!

Buffalo Chicken Salad

Grill chicken, cutting it into bite sized pieces. Toss in Buffalo sauce.

Top salads with chicken and hand cut French fries. Dress it. Don't leave it naked! Eat!

Steak Salad

Blackened or grilled as in chicken salads. Use Delmonico steaks and cut up in bite-sized chunks.

NOTE: Blacken your skillet outside on the grill. Do NOT blacken in your kitchen. You will fill the kitchen up with smoke.

Surf & Turf Salad

Top Pam's basic salad, minus the beets, with your favorite steak and imitation crab meat.

Pam's salads are so popular around Uniontown that people drive around dreaming about them.

Taco Salad

- Brown hamburger and drain fat.

- Add one or two jars of taco sauce. Stir until warm.

- Put in bowl - 3 or 4 taco shells – broken up.

- Top broken shells with lettuce, tomatoes, black olives, banana pepper rings, taco meat, shredded cheese, sour cream and salsa.

Cole Slaw

- Shred cabbage and carrots.

- Add mayonnaise, red wine vinegar, sugar and pepper to taste.

Broccoli Salad

- Cut four heads of broccoli - bite-sized

- 1 $\frac{1}{4}$ cup shredded carrots

- $\frac{1}{2}$ medium red onion – diced fine

- 3 cups shredded Cheddar cheese

- 1 $\frac{1}{2}$ qts. ®Hellman mayonnaise

- 1 $\frac{1}{2}$ lbs.crispy crumbled bacon

- 1 cup sugar

- $\frac{1}{4}$ cup red wine vinegar

- Mix well and chill.

Potato Salad

- 5 lbs. Yukon Gold potatoes – cooked and cut up into bite-sized pieces
- ½ dozen eggs – boiled and chopped
- 8 Kosher Dill pickles (Aunt Janes) diced
- ½ small onion if desired – diced
- dab mustard
- Hellman Mayonnaise
- ¼ - ½ cup sugar
- pepper, salt

Mix all together and stir well.

Macaroni Salad

Same as potato salad, but replace potatoes with macaroni. Add celery seed to taste.

Pam's House Salad Dressing

- 3 qts. red wine vinegar

- 1 qt. vegetable oil

- Handful of garlic cloves - peeled

- 4 oz. Italian seasoning

- 4 good shakes of granulated garlic

- 4 good shakes of black pepper

- 10 packets (like in the restaurant) ®Sweet and Low

Mix all. YUM!

I don't like food that's too carefully arranged; it makes me think that the chef is spending too much time arranging and not enough time cooking. If I wanted a picture I'd buy a painting.

– **Andy Rooney**

Sandwiches

Is that Pam's Prime Rib in that bun?

Blackened Prime Rib Sandwich

- Slice cold prime rib to $\frac{1}{4}$ inch thickness.

- Blacken on each side in hot cast iron skillet (outside on your grill-not inside).

- Serve on grilled sub roll with mayo, lettuce and tomato.

NOTES...

Bender Burger

- Grill two 5.3 oz. hamburger patties to perfection. Melt a slice of American cheese on each burger.

- Dress grilled sub roll with lettuce, onion and mayonnaise.

- ## Mushroom Burger

- Grill a 5.3 oz. hamburger pattie

- Saute sliced button mushrooms

- Top burger with mushrooms and Swiss cheese. Cover to melt cheese

- Cut in half and serve on sub roll with favorite toppings

Pizza Burger

- Grill a 5.3 oz. hamburger

- Top with Pam's Spaghetti Sauce and melt provolone cheese atop it.

Cut in half and serve on grilled sub roll.

Chicken Sandwich

Grilled, Blackened, Crispy or Buffalo

- See Chicken Salads. Do not cut the chicken in bite-sized pieces. Use bun or bread of your choice and favorite toppings.

Combination

- 1 egg
- 5 oz. sliced ham, 3 strips crispy bacon
- American Cheese slices

Break egg on grill and turn over when cooked almost through. Brown ham on grill. Melt cheese on top of it. Toast thick, 3-piece bread. Stack egg, ham, bacon, and cheese on bottom slice. Top with middle slice. Add lettuce and tomato. Top with third slice after applying mayonnaise. Use 4 toothpicks to hold together. Slice in four parts.

Cooking is like love. It should be entered into with abandon or not at all.

— **Harriet van Horne**

Italian Sub

* Layer sliced deli ham, salami and American cheese on grilled sub roll.

* Broil one minute to melt cheese.

* Top with lettuce and tomato and Italian dressing.

Jumbo Fish Sub

* Drop breaded 8 oz. Cod filet into frying oil. Cook for 5-7 minutes.

* Serve on rolled sub roll with tartar sauce and lettuce.

* Some love to melt cheddar on the fish. You can lay the fried fish on the grill, top it with s slices of Cheddar and cover to melt – one or two minutes.

This sandwich is a favorite of Pam's clientele.

Meatball Sub

- Heat 3 of Pam's Meatballs thoroughly in her sauce while grilling a sub roll. Top with provolone cheese. Let melt. Add to bun and enjoy yourself!

Monte Cristo

- 4 oz. thinly sliced deli ham
- 4-5 oz. sliced turkey breast
- Two slices Swiss cheese
- Two slices thick bread
- One egg, whipped

Immerge bread into egg and grill on both sides. Grill ham and turkey. Melt Swiss on meat. Top bread with meat and cheese, let and tomato. Apply mayonnaise to other slice of bread and place a top sandwich. Slice in half.

Roast Beef & Cheddar

- Simple and delicious, take 54 oz. Of thinly sliced roast beef and toss it on the grill.

- Turn when heated through and top with two slices of Cheddar cheese. Cover to melt cheese while grilling open sub roll.

- Spread roll with horseradish sauce and add roast beef and cheddar. Slice and dig in! Of course, you could add lettuce so you are getting your vegetables.

Reuben

- 5 oz. thinly sliced corn beef or turkey

- Two slices Swiss cheese

- Two slices rye or marbled rye bread

- Small portion of sauerkraut

- Thousand Island dressing

Stack corn beef or turkey, kraut and cheese on grill to heat through. Place between slices of buttered bread and grill each side.

Steak Sandwiches

- 5 oz. sliced steak

- Dices onions, green peppers and sliced mushrooms

- Provolone cheese – 2 slices

- Sub roll sliced open

On grill heat steak and saute vegetables. Top meat with vegetables and cheese. Place on bun with mayonnaise, lettuce and tomato.

Cooking is like love. It should be entered into with abandon or not at all.

— **Harriet van Horne**

Entrees

Strange to see how a good dinner and feasting reconciles everybody.
-**Samuel Pepys**

Bake a Ham Like Pam

- Use a half or whole ham. Cover with water halfway in roaster. Add 2 lb. brown sugar.

- Add 16 oz. can of pineapple rings to water.

- Add water (as it evaporates.) Keep basting during roasting.

- Start out at 400 degrees for 2 hours, then 300 degrees for three hours.

- It will fall apart.

BBQ Ribs

- Start with a full rack of baby rack ribs.

- Par boil ribs. Bring to boil. Remove from water. Put in pan with your favorite BBQ sauce. Cover with saran wrap, then top with aluminum foil.

- Bake at 350 degrees for 1 hour. Eat!

Breaded Shrimp

- Use large 16-20 size shrimp.

- Peel and de-vein.

- Split shrimp open without cutting through them all the way.

- Dip in flour, then egg wash, then Panko bread crumbs.

- NOTE: You may add coconut to bread crumbs to make coconut shrimp.

- Deep fry in 350 degree oil until golden brown. DO NOT cook longer than 5 minutes.

A man may be a pessimistic determinist before lunch and an optimist after it.

— **Aldous Huxleyn**

Chicken Cordon Bleu

- Pound out two whole boneless chicken breasts. Cut in half.

- Use one lb. of thinly sliced baked ham.

- Use one 8 oz. block of Swiss cheese. Cut into 4 - $\frac{1}{2}$ inch thick sticks.

- Flour chicken on outer side. Top with ham.

- Place cheese stick and 1/4th of a stick of butter on ham.

- Roll up, trying to close the sides (like you are rolling a tortilla)

- Place all four roll-ups in greased casserole.

- Add a stick of butter to casserole. As chicken bakes, baste with butter drippings.

- Bake at 350 degrees for 45 minutes.

Chicken Marsala

- Use sweet Marsala wine from the liquor store. Do NOT use Marsala wine from the grocery store. You will not get the same taste at all.

- Use one whole boneless chicken breast. Pound it out.

- Flour on both sides. Saute in skillet in butter over medium heat for 20 minutes.

- Slice desired amount of mushrooms, 10 – 12.

- Add mushrooms and saute until tender.

- Turn heat up to high. Pour about four shots of Marsala wine over recipe in skillet and let flame. Add more wine if needed to glaze chicken.

- Chicken should be golden and glazed.

Chicken Parmesan

- Pound out a chicken breast and coat in flour, then egg wash and bread crumbs.

- Saute in skillet in butter until golden. Add a little water to skillet. Cook through - $\frac{1}{2}$ hour or so.

- Top with provolone cheese. Cover and melt it on. Serve with side of spaghetti and Pam's sauce.

Pam's Creole Sauce is one of my favorite recipes. She used to make Omelettes for Jimmy and I in the mornings after we had all been out the night before. They were huge like many of Pam's portions, and made us so happy that I am still smiling. This year, I am making Creole for Christmas. I have never made it before. Thanks, Pammy.

Creole Sauce

- In large stock pot: 2 medium sized carrots sliced thin. Julianne 1 red pepper, one green pepper and one medium onion. Add a 12 oz. package of fresh sliced mushrooms and two medium sized zucchinis-cut in chunks.

- Add a palmful of basil, a palmful of oregano, and salt and pepper to taste. Add a tablespoon of granulated garlic. Add 2-3 tablespoons of crushed red pepper seeds to taste. Optional: cayenne pepper and/or white pepper to taste.

- Simmer until vegetables are tender.

- Add two large cans (32 oz. Cans) diced tomatoes AND two 32 oz. Cans ®Gia LaRussa Italian Sauce.

- Heat through

Serve with breaded chicken, blackened fish, in an Omelette, on rice, over shrimp. Use your imagination with this delicious Creole.

Cajun Seafood Fettuccine

- Boil water and fettuccine

- Put a quart of heavy whipping cream into skillet. Simmer on medium heat and add 1/8 cup of Cajun seasoning. Stir and heat through as it thickens.

- Add large sea scallops. Simmer 5 minutes, then add shrimp and simmer five minutes.

Fettuccine Alfredo

- Boil large pot of water and add one pound of Fettuccine noodles. Cook according to package.

- Heat heavy whipping cream in skillet, adding grated Romano cheese to preferred thickness stirring in granulated garlic to taste.

- Pour sauce over drained Fettuccine. Eat!

Chicken & Mushroom Alfredo

- Saute chicken breast. Ccut into bite-sized pieces until almost done. Add sliced mushrooms. Saute. Add heavy whipping cream, Romano and granulated garlic. Stir until warm, bubbly and to your preferred thickness.

Chicken & Broccoli Alfredo

- Saute chicken breast and broccoli as in Chicken and Mushroom Alfredo and add to Alfredo sauce.

Seafood Alfredo

- Add Sea scallops to heavy whipping cream in skillet and cook for about 5 minutes. Add large shrimp, then Romano and granulated garlic. Simmer 5 minutes at most.

Serve all the Alfredo dishes over cooked Fettuccine noodles. There is no better Alfredo sauce in the world.

Liver & Onions

- Saute as many onions in butter as you prefer.

- Use a thin beef liver. Flour on both sides.

- Fry it in butter on medium high heat on both sides quite quickly. Keep flipping it. Once there is no blood running out, it is done.

- Top with gravy.

One cannot think well, love well, sleep well, if one has not dined well.

— **Virginia Woolf**

Pam's Prime Rib – Heaven!

- 15 lb. whole boneless Rib Eye

- 1 lb. jar of paste beef base

- 32 oz. jar minced garlic in water

- 7 $\frac{1}{2}$ oz bottle Worcester Sauce

- Open meat package. Rinse off. Pat dry.

- Put beef base in microwave for 45 seconds. Spread base all over meat.

- Spread minced garlic over base.

- Let sit 5 – 10 minutes to soak up garlic.

- Pour Worcester Sauce over meat.

- Place in 250 degree oven for 3 hours.

- This will be rare.

- You will never eat better Prime Rib!

Au Jus Sauce

- Stir beef base into water warm. Heat.

- Dip slices of Prime Rib into au jus to cook more than rare: 30 seconds in boiling au jus for Medium Rare, 90 seconds for Medium.

Pittsburgh Steak

- 14oz. Rib Eye

- Rub with olive oil on both sides.

- Mix black pepper and granulated garlic. Rub both sides of steak.

- Oil one side of steak and toss in a burning cast iron skillet (outside on grill!). Cook each side 3 minutes.

  NOTES: When it gets crusty it is time to flip it. Flip with stainless steel spatula. Be very careful when turning steak. Do not splash oil.

Kissing don't last: cookery do.
George Meredith

Pork Chops (Stuffed)

- Use 4 pork chops slit for stuffing.

- Use one loaf of white bread. Tear it up.

- Chop one stick of celery - fine.

- Chop one small onion - fine.

- Melt one stick of butter.

- Two eggs

- Season with a tablespoon of pepper.

- Mix thoroughly. If not moist enough, add chicken broth as needed.

- Stuff chops and cover with brown gravy. You may use instant gravy.

- Cover with ®Saran wrap and top with aluminum foil.

- Roast at 350 degrees for an hour or an hour and a half.

NOTE: The saran wrap steams the meat, helping it cook faster and keeps it moist.

Pork Cutlets

- Use boneless pork chops. Pound them out.

- Roll in flour, then egg wash, then Italian bread crumbs.

- Brown in butter in skillet on both sides.

- Add water.

- Cover with lid to steam. Cook 1 – 1 1/2 hours. Add water as needed.

Roast a Turkey Like Pam

- Use a 20 lb. Turkey

- Stuff and roast overnight at 200 degrees.

- Add as much water as possible to roaster without making it splash out.

- Baste all morning until serving time.

Scallops

- Use jumbo Sea scallops. Do NOT use Bay scallops.

- Toss in flour. Shake off excess flour.

- Melt butter in skillet on medium high. Drop scallops in skillet.

- Add two teaspoons minced garlic. Brown on both sides. Hit with a couple shots of dry white wine. Chablis works well.

There is no sincerer love than the love of food.

— **George Bernard Shaw**

—

Spaghetti Sauce

- Use a pound of pork butt or boneless pork loin. Brown chunk of pork on all sides in enough vegetable oil to coat bottom of stock pot.

- Use large jar of any flavor of ®Ragu Spaghetti Sauce.

- Add two large cans of Del LaRussa Italian Sauce. Add one can of water.

- Add one large can of tomato paste. Stir.

- Julianne one red pepper and one green pepper. Add to sauce.

- Slice up 8 oz. of fresh mushrooms. Add.

- Season with a palmful each of Italian seasoning, oregano, and basil.

- Cook and stir on medium heat for about 45 minutes until bubbling. Turn down to a simmer. Simmer four hours.

Meatballs

- Mix together four pounds of ground chuck, salt and pepper to taste, three tablespoons of minced garlic in water, two eggs, $\frac{1}{2}$ cup ketchup, and a cup of Italian style bread crumbs.

- Roll into balls. Brown on all sides on medium high heat. Add a little water and cover. Simmer to cook through.

- Drain meatballs and add to sauce.

After a full belly all is poetry.

– **Frank McCourt**

Veal Marsala

Same as Chicken Marsala except: When you flip the veal, add the mushrooms. Veal only takes about 5 minutes on high. Longer cooking will make it tough.

Veal Parmesan

- Same as Chicken Parmesan but be aware that it cooks faster.

Veal Roulade

- Filling: Use one pound of crab meat, either lump or special.

- Add one egg to crab meat.

- Add a teaspoon of dry mustard, $\frac{1}{2}$ teaspoon of granulated garlic and approximately $\frac{1}{2}$ cup of mayonnaise.

- Add Italian bread crumbs so that the filling sticks together-about one cup. Mix well.

- Pound out 1 lb. of veal cutlet. Cut into 3-4 inch-wide strips.

- Place crab meat filling into each strip and roll. Use toothpicks to hold closed.

- Roll in flour, egg wash, then bread crumbs until covered.

- Brown in medium high skillet in butter on all sides until lightly brown color.

- Top with Alfredo sauce. This dish pairs well with Fettuccine Alfredo.

Tuna Casserole

- Boil a 12 oz. package of noodles in water.

- Drain.

- Two cans of ®Campbell cream of mushroom soup. One can of milk.

- One 12 oz. can Albacore tuna.

- One 8 oz. bag of shredded Cheddar cheese.

- One 16 oz. can of peas, drained.

- Mix all together and bake in casserole for 30 minutes. 350 degrees.

It's a Party

Food should be fun.

– **Thomas Keller**

Crab Ball

- Three lbs. cream cheese

- One lb. canned crab meat

- Four shakes ®Worchestire sauce and one teaspoon granulated garlic.

- Mix all together well and form into a ball.

- Top with cocktail sauce (ketchup and fresh horseradish)

- Top with Imitation Crab Meat.

- Serve with a variety of crackers.

There are people who strictly deprive themselves of each and every eatable, drinkable, and smokeable which has in any way acquired a shady reputation. They pay this price for health. And health is all they get for it. How strange it is. It is like paying out your whole fortune for a cow that has gone dry.

— **Mark Twain**

Taco Dip

- Brown four lbs. of hamburger and drain.

- Add one 16 oz. jar of Taco sauce to meat and let sit.

- Spread out 3 lbs. of cream cheese on an 18" round pizza pan.

- Top cheese with meat mix.

- Cover meat with chopped lettuce.

- Top with 5-6 large tomatoes, diced.

- Top with 24 oz. of shredded Cheddar cheese.

- Top all with salsa.

- Optional: Add banana pepper rings and black olives.

A good meal makes a man feel more charitable toward the world than any sermon.
Arthur Pendenys

Anyone who has ever been to Pam's Christmas parties at Bender's Pit Stop knows there are more party recipes to be had. She used to put out one heck of a spread, thanking her customers for their business.

Pam walked away from a business that got too big for her without Jimmy, BUT she will never walk away from her talent. There is only one Pam Bendishaw, and she is COOKING.

Pam Bendishaw is presently cooking at

Butch's Rainbow, Connellsville St.

Lemont Furnace, Pa. (Uniontown)

They are open Monday - Saturday, 11 a.m. - 9 p.m.

Eat-in, Take-Out, Delivery, Catering.

Call 724 439-0200

M-F Lunch Delivery to Businesses 10am – 2pm!

DAILY MENU

Appetizers

Onion Rings $3.95

Sweet Potato Fries $3.75

Breaded Mushrooms $3.75

Hot Pepper Cheese Balls $3.50

Chicken Strips 3-Piece $4.95, Add Fries $6.00

Cheese Sticks (6) $4.25

Spicy Pub Pickles (5) $4.25

Fried Zucchini   Sm. $3.95 Lg. $5.95

Soups & Chili   Cup $2.95 Bowl $3.95

Salads

House Salad $3.50

Antipasto $8.95

Chicken Salad $8.95

Blackened, Buffalo, Crispy or Grilled

Steak Salad $8.95

Surf & Turf Salad $9.95

Dressings: House Dressing, Italian, Ranch, Bleu Cheese,
Red French, Sweet & Sour, 1000 Island, Raspberry
Vinaigrette

Sandwiches - Make any sandwich a wrap!

Reuben-Corn Beef or Turkey $6.95

Steak Sandwich $7.50

Hamburger   1/3lb $4.50

Cheeseburger   1/3lb $5.50

Mushroom Burger   1/3lb $5.95

Chicken Sandwich $6.50

Roast Beef & Cheddar $5.95

Combination Club $6.50

Grilled Cheese   3.50 Add Bacon or Ham $1.50

Cod Jumbo Fish $8.95

Italian Sub $5.95

Monte Cristo $6.50

Butch's 1/4lb Hot Dog & Fries $5.95

Shaggy Dog: green peppers, onion, mushrooms, cheddar, ff and spicy ranch. Bacon Cheddar Dog, lots more. Build your own dog - 15 toppings!

Wings

$8.00 Per Dozen

Jade's Special, Hot, Mild, Hot Butter & Garlic, Butter & Garlic, Spicy Ranch, Teriyaki, BBQ, Old Bay

Dinners

Pork Cutlets $10.95

Chicken Parmesan	$12.95
Spaghetti & Meatballs	$8.95
Meatball Parmesan	$9.95
Liver & Onions	$9.95
Fettuccine Alfredo	$10.95
Add Chicken	$2.00
Fish Dinner	$12.95

Dinners include: Choice of Potato or Pasta (excluding Fettuccine)

Side Dishes

Hand Cut French Fries Sm $2.95   Lg $3.95

Side of Fettuccine Alfredo	$4.95
Pasta	$3.50
Baked Potato	$2.95
Cole Slaw	$2.00

Nightly Specials 4 - 9 p. m

Monday - Build-Your-Burger

Tuesday – Pasta Night

Wednesday – Wing Night

Thursday – Mexican Night

Friday – Fish Fry Friday!

* NO TAKE OUT on above Nightly Specials.

Friday & Saturday - Prime Rib 14oz. $16.95, 3 – 9pm

Enjoy our $6.95 Lunch Specials!

WE DELIVER Lunch to businesses within 10 miles. $2. delivery charge.

NOTE: Every Monday, we fax out our weekly lunch specials menu. Get on the list!

Call: 724 439-0200

ABOUT THE AUTHOR

Pam's Cooking is Marci McGuinness' 30th book.
More books by McGuinness:

Summit Mountain Hill Climb Program 1915 - Reprint
Murder in St. Michaels
Speedway Kings of SW PA, 100 Years of Racing History
Ohiopyle, That Little Town, WWII
Gone to Ohiopyle
Message of the Sacred Buffalo
Murder in Ohiopyle
Hauntings of Pittsburgh & the Laurel Highlands
Yesteryear at the Uniontown Speedway
Uniontown Speedway 1916 Program – Reprint
The Explorer's Guide to the Yough River & Ohiopyle
Yesteryear in Ohiopyle, Volumes I, II & III
Yesteryear in Masontown
Yesteryear in Smithfield and Point Marion
Stone House Legends and Lore
The Deer Hunter's Guide to Success
Many more!

Find McGuinness' books at Pechin in Dunbar, Rx+ in
Hopwood, Backyard Gardens in Ohiopyle,
www.amazon.com, www.ohiopyle.com,
www.uniontownspeedway.com.

Or Order by phone: 724 710-2821

www.ingramcontent.com/pod-product-compliance
Lightning Source LLC
Chambersburg PA
CBHW021911040426
42447CB00007B/801